A New True Book

RECYCLING

By Joan Kalbacken
and
Emilie U. Lepthien

CP CHILDRENS PRESS®
CHICAGO

TOPS
RECYCLING
CENTER

REUSE · REDUCE · RECYCLE

PAPER BAGS

PLASTIC BAGS

ONLY COMPLETELY EMPTY PAPER AND PLASTIC BAGS CAN BE RECYCLED

RECYCLE PAPER BAGS

RECYCL PLASTI BAGS

REUSE

Community recycling center
for paper and plastic bags

PHOTO CREDITS

© Cameramann International, Ltd.—17 (left), 18 (top left), 41 (right), 44 (bottom left)

Custom Medical Stock—© R. F. Wehr, 2; © Jon Meyer, 28 (left), 33, 44 (bottom right)

Historical Pictures Service, Chicago—© Tom Neiman—9 (left), 23

© Joan Kalbacken—4 (bottom right), 17 (bottom right), 28 (right)

© Emilie Lepthien—8 (2 photos), 35 (right), 40

Norma Morrison—10 (2 photos), 15 (right), 38 (2 photos)

Photri—27 (right); © Kulik, 43

Root Resources—© Gail Nachel, 11, 19; © Jim Nachel, 13 (right), 14 (2 photos)

Tom Stack & Associates—© Jack D. Swenson, 25 (bottom left); © R. Smith, 39 (right)

© Lynn M. Stone—4 (bottom left), 15 (left), 21 (right)

SuperStock International, Inc.—© William Hamilton, 25 (right)

TSW/CLICK-Chicago—© Steve Elmore, Cover, 30; © Gerald Herbeck, 9 (right); © Chuck Keeler, 12 (right); © Don & Pat Valenti, 17 (top right)

Valan—© V. Wilkinson, 4 (top), 13 (left), 21 (left), 27 (left), 31, 37, 39 (left); © Halle Flygare, 7; © J. A. Wilkinson, 12 (left); © B. Templeman, 18 (top right); © Pierre Kohlet, 18 (bottom right); © Joyce Photographics, 18 (bottom left), 25 (top left); © Phillip Norton, 35 (left); © R. Moller, 41 (left); © Chris Malazdrewicz, 44 (top)

Cover — Cans and bottles sorted for recycling

Library of Congress Cataloging-in-Publication Data

Kalbacken, Joan.
  Recycling / by Joan Kalbacken and Emilie U. Lepthien.
     p.   cm. — (A New true book)
  Includes index.
  Summary: Shows how the ever-growing tide of refuse threatens the environment and wastes resources, and how recycling helps in conservation efforts.
  ISBN 0-516-01118-9
  1. Recycling (Waste, etc.)—Juvenile literature.
[1. Recycling (Waste)] I. Lepthien, Emilie U. (Emilie Utteg) II. Title.
TD794.5.K35 1991   90-21275
363.72'82—dc20   CIP
                                          AC

TABLE OF CONTENTS

The mountains of paper products (above), plastic containers
(below left), and beverage cans (below right) that we use
every year can be recycled and their materials used again.

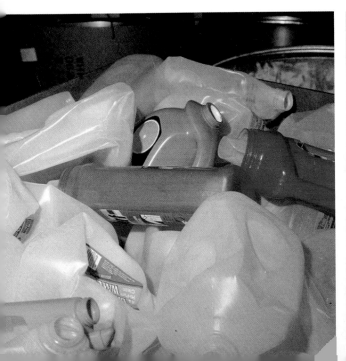 

MOUNTAINS OF GARBAGE

The world is running out of garbage dumps. This has come about because people have been wasteful. Every day, we waste wood products, metals, glass, plastics, and energy.

The good news is that people are changing. They are reusing things they used to throw away. Using products over again is called recycling. Recycling saves not only materials and energy, but also space in landfills.

Many countries have a problem finding a place for their garbage. In the United States at least 162 million tons of garbage are collected each year. This garbage would fill 1,000 football fields piled thirty stories high. Each American throws away four to six pounds of garbage every day. There is so much garbage that soon there will be no place to dump it.

A garbage truck dumps its load into a sanitary landfill.

LANDFILLS

Landfills are places where garbage is dumped. In "sanitary" landfills the garbage is covered with soil. The garbage under the soil does not decompose, or break down, for a long time. Some of it will never decompose.

7

Many things that are put
into landfills can be recycled.
Newspapers, aluminum, plastics,
glass, and other materials
can be made into new useful
items. Today, only one-tenth of
North America's waste is being
recycled, although more than
half of the garbage could
be recycled.

Note cards (left) showing endangered species are printed on recycled paper.
Playground equipment (right) made from recycled plastic

PAPER

Newspapers make up a large part of our garbage. Newsprint—the paper on which newspapers are printed—is made from wood pulp, which comes from trees.

If all the Sunday papers in North America were

A man picks up newspapers (right) to deliver to a recycling center (left).

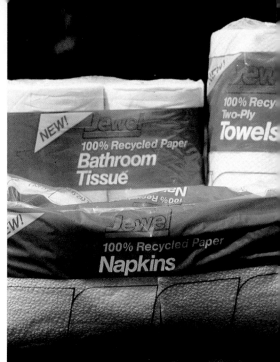

The newspapers at this recycling center (left)
will be turned into paper products (right).

recycled, more than 500,000
trees a week would be
saved. Recycled newsprint
is used again to print
newspapers. It is also
made into insulation, boxboard,
and other paper products.

10

A pet guinea pig beds down in shredded newspaper.

Shredded newsprint makes good animal bedding too. Farmers like it better than straw for their livestock. More newspaper recycling mills are needed.

Businesses and offices use thousands of tons of paper every year. The all-white paper and computer

Computer printouts (above) and shredded paper (right) from offices make the best recycled paper products.

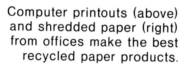

printouts used in offices are the highest-quality papers that are made. This high-quality paper makes the best recycled paper products. Before recycling, however, this paper must be separated from newsprint.

CARDBOARD

There are two kinds of cardboard: corrugated cardboard and paperboard. Corrugated cardboard is a sandwich of two sheets of cardboard with grooved paper between them.

Unlike corrugated cardboard, paperboard can

Corrugated cardboard (below) resembles a sandwich. This symbol (right) appears on recycled corrugated cardboard.

Corrugated Recycles

easily be folded by hand. It is made of only one layer of cardboard. It can also be recycled. Many supermarket products come in recycled paperboard. Such items are packed in boxes stamped with a symbol and the words "packaged in recycled paperboard."

Paperboard (left) awaiting recycling. Look for the recycled message and symbol (right) on household products.

WARRANTY TO CONSUMERS
★
od Housekeeping
PROMISES
CEMENT OR REFUND IF DEFECTIVE

If you have questions or comments
ZIPLOC Brand Freezer Bags, plea
call us TOLL FREE 1-800-428-47

hen writing us concerning this product, please en
sample bag and this complete bottom panel of th

Packaged in recycled paperboard. ZIPL
are made from polyethylene, a recycl
photodegradable material. Please dis
properly to prevent litter.

Aluminum cans at a recycling center

ALUMINUM

Aluminum is one of the easiest materials to recycle. More than 95 percent of all canned drinks are sold in aluminum cans. Used aluminum cans can be recycled and made into new cans.

15

Most aluminum is made from an ore called bauxite. The United States imports bauxite from other countries. This costs a great deal of money. And it takes a lot of energy to process aluminum from bauxite ore. That energy is also expensive. When aluminum is recycled, however, 95 percent of the energy it takes to make new aluminum is saved.

Recycling centers pay millions of dollars to children

Aluminum cans are paid
for by weight at some
recycling centers.

and adults for collecting
aluminum cans, aluminum
foil, and other aluminum
products. And aluminum can
be used over and over again.
It is the perfect material for
recycling.

Aluminum can be used to make everything from Little League baseball bats to space vehicles. Because it is lightweight, strong, and durable, aluminum is also important in building ships, airplanes, trucks, trains, cars, and even skyscrapers.

OTHER METALS

Many foods are sold in cans. These cans are made of steel coated with a thin layer of tin. The tin must be separated from the steel before these two metals can be recycled.

The steel and tin in these cans will be recycled into new products.

Almost 3 million tons of these cans are discarded every year. Recycled steel can be used to make new steel. Recycled tin can be made into new tin products.

Tin ore is not mined in North America. It is expensive to import tin. But, unfortunately, not every recycling center accepts "tin" cans. And these cans take 100 years to decompose in a landfill.

GLASS

For many years, milk was sold in glass bottles. The empty bottles were returned to the dairy to be sterilized and refilled. This process was a form of recycling.

Glass does not decompose in landfills. To save space in landfills, some states have laws that require a deposit on glass beverage bottles.

The money is refunded when people return the empty bottles to be recycled.

All glass can be recycled. Making new bottles and jars from old glass costs less than manufacturing them from raw materials. It saves energy, too.

The average household buys about 150 glass containers every year. Only about 10 percent of these glass containers are recycled. Glass manufacturers

Glass containers must be separated by color for recycling.

pay people to return glass.
Used glass is then separated
by color at recycling
collection centers.

Recycling the paper,
aluminum cans, and glass in
a household's garbage
would reduce the amount of
garbage by about 25 percent.

PLASTICS

Plastic is used to make many products. Almost 60 billion pounds of plastic is produced every year and about 25 percent is used in food packaging.

Unfortunately, plastic waste pollutes beaches and often traps wildlife. As many as 2 million birds and more than 100,000 mammals are killed each year by this discarded plastic. Seabirds, seals, turtles, dolphins, and

Wildlife victims of discarded plastics: A fish caught in a plastic ring (top left), a sea lion whose neck is encircled by a fishing net (bottom left), and a pelican killed by fishing line (above).

other sea animals are trapped in plastic nets, fishing lines, bags, and beverage-can rings. People must dispose of plastic materials more carefully to protect wildlife.

Plastics are made from petroleum, resins, and vegetable products. Scientists have long worked to make plastics more durable. Now they are working to make these materials decompose more quickly. One-third of landfill space is filled with plastics today. Plastic bags take from ten to twenty years to decompose in a landfill. Other containers may take nearly one hundred years. Plastic-foam cups, plates,

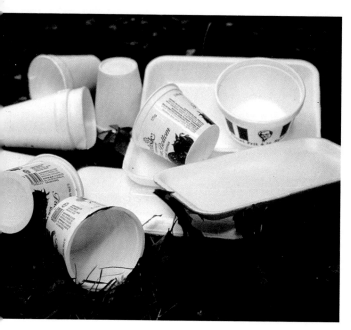

Plastic-foam food containers (left) will never decompose.
But the milk carton (right) is completely degradable.

and fast-food boxes will
never decompose.

Some companies are now
manufacturing "degradable"
plastics. Degradable
plastics decompose easily.
However, even degradable
plastics do not decompose

A collection box for used plastic bags (left). Plastic beverage bottles (right) must be sorted according to color and type for recycling.

quickly in landfills, which lack the right moisture, air, and temperature.

Supermarkets today are asking customers to return their plastic shopping bags for recycling. These bags can be burned — they do not give off toxic (dangerous) gases. Many plastics cannot be burned because they give off toxic gases that pollute the air.

In most recycling processes, the plastics must be sorted according to color and type of plastic before they are cleaned and reprocessed. Sorting and cleaning make the process very expensive.

However, a recycling process has been developed that mixes all kinds and colors of plastic. This

A plastic recycling plant in Allentown, Pennsylvania

process is less costly.

Park benches, playground equipment, and landscape timbers are made from recycled plastic. Plastic landscape timbers are expected to last about 400 years. And, since these plastic items can be made in colors, they do not need to be painted.

OIL

This dirty motor oil can be cleaned and used again.

Motor oil does not wear out—it only becomes dirty with use. More than half of the people who own cars, trucks, and tractors change their own motor oil. In one year 400 million gallons of this dirty oil is dumped on the ground, poured down

31

sewers, or thrown in landfills. When used oil seeps into the ground, it pollutes wells, rivers, and lakes.

People who dump oil carelessly waste a valuable natural resource and increase the country's dependence on imported oil. The motor oil that is carelessly dumped every year would generate enough electricity to supply 360,000 homes.

Dirty oil can be recycled. When the dirt and impurities

Used oil is collected at some gas stations for recycling.

are removed, the oil can be used again.

Some service stations have areas where people can bring their used oil in clean plastic containers to be picked up for recycling.

TIRES

Over 200 million worn-out tires are thrown away each year in North America. Most of them are steel-belted tires, made of rubber, chemicals, and steel. Not enough of these tires are being recycled. Instead, they are building up in huge piles that are harmful to the environment.

About 35 percent of truck tires and 5 to 10 percent of automobile tires are recapped,

These used tires (left) can be recycled into many useful rubber products. A worker (right) attaches new treads to a truck tire.

or given new treads. Then the tires can be used again.

In some recycling factories, discarded tires are shredded or chipped, and big magnets remove the steel particles. The chipped rubber can then be mixed with asphalt to make airport runways, running tracks, and highways where the surface must be softer or more flexible.

Recycled rubber is also made into doormats for the entrances of many public buildings such as schools and offices. Chipped rubber is burned to heat cement kilns. Many other uses have been found for worn-out tires. Tire manufacturers are becoming more and more interested in recycling.

YARD WASTE

An average of 18 percent of solid waste comes from grass clippings, leaves, tree trimmings, and brush.

Homeowners can reduce this amount and also improve their gardens by "composting." Today, many communities have composting centers.

Many communities no longer accept yard waste in garbage pickups. These grass cuttings and leaves can be composted and used as fertilizer.

Gardeners (left) adding yard waste to the compost pile. Finished compost (right) makes an excellent fertilizer and soil conditioner.

In composting, grass clippings and leaves are heaped in piles. These piles decay within a few months and form a mixture—or compost—that enriches garden soil. Yard waste spread around garden plants also controls weeds.

Many cities collect
discarded Christmas trees
and use the needles and
chipped trunks and branches
to make mulch. The mulch
is then placed around trees
and shrubs to protect the
plants and enrich the soil.

Left: Mulch on celery plants. Right: Recycling Christmas trees

FROM WASTE TO ELECTRICITY

In some communities garbage is burned in large furnaces called incinerators. Some cities in North America and other countries incinerate (burn) garbage to generate electricity. The

Solid waste is burned in this plant to generate electricity.

Energy to heat and light many homes comes from
electricity generated by burning solid waste.

electricity is then used to
heat and light many homes.
    Engineers and scientists
are working to reduce the air
pollution caused by the
gases and ash given off by
burning garbage.

MAKING A HABIT OF RECYCLING

Today, many communities and states have laws requiring people to separate their garbage. Some communities have drop-off centers that collect recyclable materials. In other places, the community provides containers that enable people to separate their own newspapers, plastics, aluminum, and glass for collection.

A recycling exhibit in Washington, D.C., on Earth Day, April 22, 1990.

Some cities hold fairs where people learn more about the importance of recycling. The fairs have exhibits of recycled products. They show how much recycling benefits our environment.

Industrialized countries must find new ways to cope with their millions of tons of garbage before we run out of space for landfills.

Schools and youth groups often conduct paper drives or collect glass and aluminum as fund-raising projects. They may use the money to buy school equipment, pay for field trips, or help needy people.

Unless Americans learn to recycle their garbage, the country will run out of landfills. There may not be enough places to bury garbage by the end of the twentieth century.

WORDS YOU SHOULD KNOW

asphalt (AS • fawlt) — a dark, sticky substance that is mixed with sand and gravel and used to pave roads

bauxite (BOX • ite) — a claylike substance that contains aluminum

composting (KAHM • poh • sting) — allowing grass clippings, leaves, and other plant parts to decay into a substance that fertilizes soil

corrugated (KOR • ih • gayt • ed) — having grooves and ridges

decompose (dee • kum • POHZ) — to break down into separate parts; to rot or decay

degradable (dih • GRAY • dih • bil) — able to decompose

durable (DOO • rih • bil) — long-lasting; not easily decomposed

energy (EN • er • gee) — the ability to do work; the work supplied by fuels such as coal and oil

environment (en • VY • ron • mint) — the things that surround anything; the air, soil, water, etc.

flexible (FLEX • ih • bil) — able to bend easily

generate (JEN • er • ayt) — to give rise to; to make or create

impurities (im • PYOOR • ih • teez) — things such as chemicals or particles that make something dirty

incinerator (in • SIN • er • ray • ter) — a furnace that is used to burn garbage

insulation (in • suh • LAY • shun) — a substance that helps hold in heat

landfill (LAND • fill) — a place where garbage is dumped

magnet (MAG • nit) — a piece of iron or steel that has the power to draw iron or some other metal to it

mulch (MUHLCH) — a layer of wood chips, compost, or other organic matter spread around trees and in gardens to help condition the soil and hold in moisture

pollute (puh • LOOT) — to make dirty
resin (REH • zin) — a sticky substance found inside certain trees and other plants
sterilized (STIR • ih • lyzed) — made germ-free by heating
toxic (TAHX • ik) — poisonous; harmful to living things

INDEX

About the Authors

Joan Formell Kalbacken earned a BA in Education from the University of Wisconsin, Madison. After graduate work at Coe College, Iowa, and the University of Toulouse, France, she received an MA from Illinois State University, Normal, Illinois. She was a secondary school teacher in Beloit, Wisconsin, and Pekin and Normal, Illinois. She taught French and mathematics for twenty-nine years and she also served as foreign language supervisor in Normal. She received the award for excellence in Illinois' program, "Those Who Excel."

She is past state president of the Delta Kappa Gamma Society International and a member of Pi Delta Phi, Kappa Delta Pi, AAUW, and Phi Delta Kappa.

Emilie U. Lepthien received her BA and MS degrees and certificate in school administration from Northwestern University. She taught upper grade science and social studies, wrote and narrated science programs for the Chicago Public Schools' station WBEZ, and was principal in Chicago, Illinois for twenty years. She received the American Educator's Medal from Freedoms Foundation.

She is a member of Delta Kappa Gamma Society International, Chicago Principals' Association, Illinois Women's Press Association, National Federation of Press Women, and AAUW.

She has written books in the Enchantment of the World, New True Books, and America the Beautiful series.

48